T0157509

Sunflower

A Flow To Light

ANITA DENEAULT

BALBOA.
PRESS

A DIVISION OF HAY HOUSE

Balboa Press books may be ordered through booksellers or by contacting:

Balboa Press
A Division of Hay House
1663 Liberty Drive
Bloomington, IN 47403
www.balboapress.com
1 (877) 407-4847

Because of the dynamic nature of the Internet, any web addresses or links contained in this book may have changed since publication and may no longer be valid. The views expressed in this work are solely those of the author and do not necessarily reflect the views of the publisher, and the publisher hereby disclaims any responsibility for them.

The author of this book does not dispense medical advice or prescribe the use of any technique as a form of treatment for physical, emotional, or medical problems without the advice of a physician, either directly or indirectly. The intent of the author is only to offer information of a general nature to help you in your quest for emotional and spiritual well-being. In the event you use any of the information in this book for yourself, which is your constitutional right, the author and the publisher assume no responsibility for your actions.

Any people depicted in stock imagery provided by Thinkstock are models, and such images are being used for illustrative purposes only. Certain stock imagery © Thinkstock.

Print information available on the last page.

ISBN: 978-1-5043-6215-3 (sc)
ISBN: 978-1-5043-6220-7 (e)

Library of Congress Control Number: 2016911325

Balboa Press rev. date: 09/12/2016

Contents

All to the Best

Sitting here after knowing my book has been put
out there, I do not know where it will end up.
I recognize that it has been a journey, not only for the
book to realize its potential but also for me to have
journeyed far enough to allow it to be released.
It has been a journey of peeking at my potential
and looking to smile back at it or to finger it.
It all came at a cost, really. It was a little bit of
freedom to realize the book's worth, to let it go.
As with my writing, my life and my relationships, each
experience has developed me into the human that you see today.
I am absolutely honoured to share my journey. I know it is my
life's purpose that I will hold, love, nurture, cherish and honour.
Great Spirit, Guides, Angels, Deities, Ascended
Masters and passed loved ones, *kukwstsemc*
(thank you). I am blessed and happy.
Great Spirit, we had it right: we are Here.
And I will be here to do this work along with you and all those
who love, cherish, protect and aid me in my advancement.
I can match it now.
It is a journey, a privilege, a right.

Sitting on a Sunflower

Singin' Here,
Lovin' there.
Optimistically placed in life.
Cherished in that,
Placed over this,
Wanting more of that.
Creating a missed this,
Letting go of that.
Hoping with this,
Cherishing that.
So as I cherish and hope, I see up on the moon.
As I pray, I say this to that bolt, this over to
that, from this to that and then to me.
So as I meet and beat those next moments of
thought and high jump over them, I giggle.
I giggle because I am sitting with this, watching
that, creating a space in this and being optimistic
about that—well, that becomes the Dream,
A dream to maneuver and still hold,
Hold to the moment,
This prized steer of a moment.
Sitting with a moment that is just that, withholding
my expectation and wishing less on that.
So as I withhold, sit, and stare, and experience
this moment, I just sit and just stare.
This moment shifts this, elevates that
and opens up that other thing.
So when it all becomes unravelled and perfect, according
to the One's plan, I smile because, well, it has all settled.

So as I sit in this settled spot, I just sit.
I just sit to find the space to smile some more—
More sitting, less doing and a lot of enjoying.
Today I will follow the Sunflower's
example and pivot to the Light.
Today I will just marvel at the sunflower's
beauty, simplicity, wise pose and direction.
So with this view, with this moment and with this time, I Smile!

A Great Dream and
an Amazing Sail

Hoping, blowing, clueing and pursing a new view.
Feeling a breeze upon my cheeks, feeling the
wind brush gently across my hair.
Feel it all as I close my eyes and see.
See the ocean open up and bob me up and down.
Feel as I see the horizon and blanket myself in its peace.
Feel as I am held by the man I adore.
Feel it as my partner and life walker wraps his
strong and loving arms around me.
Feel as the spirit in each of us mixes in a kiss.
Feel as the calm starts to wash down my arms
and moves to the tips of my toes.
Feel as this moment tickles and kisses my heart.
It is a Peace-filled bliss.
Feel as I nestle deeper into his arms.
Feel secure in this moment. It is then that I
open myself up to this time and space.
Feel as I enjoy it.
Feel as I enjoy and taste the salt on my lip.
Feel as I am quivering in anticipation for life's next moment
in this space with a man I love and adore, a man whom I
have come to appreciate with crystal-clear appreciation!

An Angel's Presence

There was a large gathering of people. A few were at the side.
It was a big building, and those who were on
the side were facing a possessed person.
As I was in the middle, we all prayed and
chanted to get rid of this being.
It was kept at bay as we chanted and prayed,
but it did not leave quite yet.
It was in that moment that I noticed a
person was walking toward me
I could feel her power.
She had white hair and was dressed in white.
I never looked at her features, and I don't remember what she
looked like, but I do remember her soft, consistent demeanour.
I am referring to this person as a woman, but I
do not think it was a man or a woman.
As she approached this wicked being, I saw it shriek away.
Her powerful presence lent itself to
create this creature's response.
She looked at me and said, "Be careful when this bull is
released from this person, because it is in them really deep."
I remember thinking that I did not know that it would have
been something inside the person's spirit which made this
other person's powerful presence that much more needed.
This powerful person was the direction. I remember
someone telling me, "Look, they released it."
As I looked over, I saw a big black cloud dissipating in the air.
All I remember is the powerful presence of a
woman and knowing it would all be fine.

Previous to that, I had strength and faith, but I remember being mindful of how close I had come. I knew my perseverance had to remain strong to keep this being in the middle of the people.

I am glad I had this dream, as I felt protected and I knew that all would be fine.

I liked that I witnessed something that was powerful enough to make evil back up.

I was glad that I was one of the people who aided, but I was also glad I was able to pass the matter to someone who was spiritually present, powerful and complete.

An Ocean, a Sister

It amazes me, the sensation of being in the
Moment, and how one breath, open eyes and an
open spirit can swill the Openness in me.
Walking by the ocean, I sometimes forget
how soulfully connected I am to it,
How my soul, body, mind and heart, right down to each
cell in my body, all lavish in the fulfilling beauty of it.
I absolutely cannot fathom it until I am in its presence.
Equally so, I absolutely appreciate that
I can experience and *know it*.
I was thinking of my sister today and felt how much
I absolutely cherish, love and admire her.
I cannot explain my connection to her any
more than I can explain my soulful amazement
with, and connection to, the ocean.
No matter what my love is, here I am clear, both for you,
my sister, Sarah, and for this magnificent ocean.
I am privileged to be here in this life with you.
I love you.

I've Arrived, Yea

Sitting, loving, hoping, praying.
This expansive, engulfing, huge new wave has
just washed through me and I am still here.
Well, based on my smile, I find that my humour
is still intact with this oversized flow.
Now that I sit here with a wee bit of humour, sparkling eyes
and an open demeanour, I start to wonder. But I know that
when I do this, it can create too much noise, so I look away.
I can allow it to flow past me, and I can smile at
it while it does, with the patience embedded in
the stars and with the strength of stone.
So it is in this moment that I listen to music, envisioning
myself upon an expansive cliff that overlooks a vast
ocean. It is then that I open myself up to being *here*.
I am at Peace.
So upon this cliff I sit. I know that nestled within me
is the golden glow of love, and I feel that remembrance
of safety, poise and openness that I know.
It is then that I know I have arrived again!

Boldness Crescendo to Me to Who?

Up on a hill I climb,
Passing through the sky. I am upon a bridge that
meets the me, moving to the sky to the next me.
Hear as I squirm.
I can feel the budding newness that, although I know it will
feel good later, in this moment feels like an adjustment.
I do not know where I sit, but I am sitting just the same;
Hear as I keep calling to my needs.
I keep calling as I believe.
Keep smiling when I feel my intuition
hit my present circumstances.
Feed the next level as I smile and sit purposefully in my life.
I need to sit as I hold myself up to my own potential,
Listening,
Trusting,
Believing,
Honouring myself, this life, God, Creator, Buddha,
whoever. All that I know is that I feel Him,
Cherished,
Blessed,
Created,
Purposed,
Enveloped in gold,
And becoming more subtle but feeling quite bold.

9

Broken Cages

Pushing the edges for so many years;
Seeing this edge as real.
Feel the bars surround and pinch potential.
In this moment I look closely and see how clear it is,
So as I touch through the fake,
As I grasp beyond my beliefs,
As I smile with a stepping up of my beliefs and
Arrogance, to certainty I smile again.
I smile because I know that I know. Imaginings are blank.
As I sit to reclaim the One, the bars, that
translucent cage, mirages into transparency.
Breathe.
Taste.
Smile.
Claim.
Open and smile again.
Arrogance or certainty does not much matter—it feels open.
The waiting has stopped.
Time has arrived.
Feel the openness that tastes like Forgiveness,
Success, Absolution and any other Human
Memory or _____.
Bars, cages, beliefs, toiling:
Real?
Feel the moment I touch beyond,
Nod my head,
Press my face through the Fake
And taste you;
Taste the planes that connect me to you, Creator.

Feel.

Feel it.

Feel it course through this Lady, with one
step of Absolution to Another;

Feel as Absolution in a conventional sense does not
make sense. But even as I write, a bar reappears.

How to explain *moments*?

The moment is with you, Creator, and "thank
you" is the phrase/thought here.

Cages, Mirages, shimmers—let go again.

Thank you!

Chill Brew

Cherished little baby, this one called life.
Cheering in beer as I hold it up to my
lips, sipping its golden love.
Feel the lust hit the middle from me to you.
This magical drink that sings so much of those
nestled moments is left unspoken but seems to dwell
outwardly when you touch my inner ghosts.
So as the lust and guaranteed openness remain unsaid,
that which is untapped comes to the surface. This is a
song that sometimes dwells but is left unspoken.
So as the beauty that is the known comes in contact with
the unspoken, often untreasured under the lips, those
who await it are amidst the tranquility of non-thought.
Opening to what is not said, what is best treasured in the mind
of those still seeking a voice, it sits so tranquil, untarnished with
rational thought. Open sex, creative tongues and open laughs.

Cuteness

Pondering the cuteness.

Wishing for the optional options.

Peeking to the aisle of Ones who pose and gesture to the new.

Holding my life

Holding to this life, my life.

As I hold to this, I hope.

When I hold no more, I open—and it does too.

Energy, Gem, Nuggets

I had coffee with my friend Amy. It was a day of sparkly energy.
That which I needed was received, including vitamin D,
unplugging my connection from information/space, increased
energy from meeting with her, and sharing in another
moment of trust, happiness and creativity, and openness
to a future both with life and with my dear friend Amy.
Creation of hope is lit afire and fanned with this moment.
Thank you, Creator.
The volts of Creation and connection reminded me of Me.
It is interesting that in the moment we receive,
share and are drawn to it equally.
It energizes down so that this teaching, moment
and time all become an equal share.
It is a perfect day and life, a perfect Light.
I realized I am a pride animal, because I feel the
need to share Source knowledge with others.
It is a human recollection of insight and
love that we can all share.
Pride's path opens the part of my spirit that allows it to
flow freely and to reciprocate with light and the world.
It connects me to who I am at my core, my core self.
So thank you for the shared moments, insights and options
to continue to connect with life, love and this world.

Floating

Words floating around, crashing, smashing,
kissing this one to that one,
All to no end.
Even as I smell the possible stink or lusciousness of them, I
smile or sign, depending on what I reach out to touch.
So as this language of emotion, relationships and
interactions provides, I now realize that I can choose
to grab them or leave them to float, poke, swell or
feed on this little beautiful soul called Me.
Thank you, Angels, Guides, Creator and Deities,
for this vision, as once upon a time I would have
believed each and every one of them.
I would have soaked it all in, one tear at a time, and
allowed it to impact me, scar me and hold me to it.
In turn I would have to try to shift and adapt to
it, but usually I wouldn't do this successfully.
Now that I can recognize these floating words as floating
options from others, this world or other realms that can
be picked up or left alone, the choice is always clear.
The choice is One's Divine Path, which is unmuddled with *other*.
The Choice becomes clear,
And It Is So.
Today I will look at them and will allow my own best interest,
Life, and Higher work to be the *flow* of where my life will go.
I will be completely Here and, well, everywhere.
Love it.
Thank you, Creator, Guides, Angels and Deities, for this vision.

Galloping

With my heart's book looking at the Universe,
connecting to this moment,
I have come to appreciate the flow of one moment—
crescendo, peak, and the fall that looks like a wave,
The crashing, the purging deep, the reaching
high from one idea or thought, and then the
connection to another—and then a calm rest.
I have come to appreciate the horse that gallops
to carry messages to me in one flash, the
lightning bolt that flashes the song, word, light, life,
that is transforming into this moment and the next.
Here it has arrived again.
It is here to capture me and take me to you, to the Universe,
and then from the Universe to you, and then cycling back
to me, and then repeating the process all over again.
Peace, Light.

God

Swoopin', scoopin', lifting, singing,
sittin', and singin' some more.
Feel the centre as it reaches through the
stars and nestles into my heart,
Love blossoming around and nestling,
Nestling as light as a feather swooping, gliding
and then sailing lightly to the ground.
My heart is open and peaceful.
Feel it open with a vision of places and spaces
not known prior to this moment.
Feel as one tear, and then another, falls in
appreciation of this Moment from me to you.
It feels that when I open my heart, it sits more like
a landscape than like something biological;
It feels like a picture, a moment, a space that opens so much
more potential than the one discovered not so long ago.
The repair, the peace and the Moment all sit
within, and all in this one expansive second.
As I sit, I feel.
As I feel, I see the Light that is in this Moment. The
expansive Moment is captured in this one second.
See the open landscape that holds nothing
to itself but lends itself to see it All.
To see this one pleasant second holds my heart open,
An open sensation that feels like a large opening in my chest.
Even as I breathe it feels like it is open from one end of
my shoulder to the other, which is an odd sensation,
So as I am opening, I am seeing and feeling.
As I am feeling and seeing, I am crying some more.

They are tears of joy as I feel more love, options, peace,
tranquility and openness, and an all-encompassing love.
Feel as I open more to this space, and know that
I am not in need of opening, forcing or wishing
for anything more beyond just knowing *it is*.
In this expansive view, I see you, God.
Thank you.
Thank you for showing me *more of me* and *more of you*
And *more of that* which touches, nestles and holds us.

Happy

Tickle, Tickle upon a bliss.
Trying to sit with a sunset and peek upon a cloud.
Smiling as the waves crescendo, touch my
breath and breathe into my heart.
Feel my spirit sings and welcome its visit
Feel as the cherry blossoms surround me.
Feel my smile as I admire and feel connected to the ocean.
The chatter that surrounded me before
just ain't here now. Ha-ha.
Smile in awe of it.
Smile as I feel it.
Feel the moment that is You to me.
See this as a sign.
In this moment, the tranquility and the well-
crafted individual gift is appreciated.
See and know.
As I sit and look out, the peace-washed presence
surrounds my spirit with gracious gratitude.
Awe is the answer to this moment, but I really do
not need an answer except gratitude, peace.
This touch from you to me and back
again is a spiritual connection.
It is a reminder of it all.
It is nice and appreciated.
It is funny, the depth of the love, connection and
openness, and the surprise upon feeling it once again.

In this sunset, upon this cliff, looking upon this
sight with the surge of the water I love,
I say, "*Kukwstsemc* [thank you], Creator, as I feel you—and me!"
A moment of tranquility, peace, bliss,
happiness and, hmmm, *moment*.
I am here.

Heart, Gold and Waves

Flounder, blunder, clutter.

See the peak and the opening of this cave to an expansive wave,

Peaking off the sidelines to crescent to the opening sunset,

Pouring the energy needed into the next wave.

Each opening opens and cleanses more.

The flow is a flow to the opening, to One.

Feel it peak, crescent, open some more—the lushness of it.

Feel the exotic lushness in me that

Tickles it,

Opens it,

Blossoming it open.

The waves wrap around me,

Open me more.

My heart sighs in escalation, release.

Sunlight golden, welcoming.

Heart open and moving as smoothly as the tides.

Hello, Healthy!

Hitting on a hill,
Crashing in the sand.
Doubting as the sound bridges me to you.
I see, and want to hear so much more.
Calling as the thunder crashes upon the waves
into my heart. The breaking feels slight as I
hear upon the stars your name, Chris.
I hear your voice and it tickles my heart.
Hear it as I sing to you.
Do you see me?
No.
As I hear is the sound as the message reaches me. I
look in this present reality and doubt its impact—
patience, patience, patience and love.
They all do not seem to be in this moment.
Feel the pinch and feel the squeeze in my
chest as I breathe past my own heart.
As I sing a song that dances within my heart, I sing
a song so deep that I hit a new heart note.
Even as I write, I peek at the possibility of none,
So with a little pessimism and sarcasm I smile
to the earth, to the light and to myself.
Today is a bright day with blue skies. I will sing
with my entire spirit of all that the One offers.
He will be good, honest, reflective and
gorgeous, both inside and out.
I sing to you.
I sing the song that binds us both.

I sing to the prospect and will continue to live this
gorgeous life that the Great Spirit sings to me.
So my God, my true Creator, I love you.
I do believe.
I am here and am True to it.
I can await and live out this manifested path of
wellness, beauty, trust, honesty and Belief.
I know I do believe.
As I look out at the ocean. I know the sails are
blowing and, yes, the water is calm.
Sing, my brother; sing, my friend; sing, my
lover; sing, my partner; sing to me.
Sing me a lullaby that binds us.
Sing to me as you feel my essence, my presence, my subtle
touch and my deep creation—and my devotion to the next Us.
Sing a strong song that rings us to us and to everything,
as we will create with and in one another.
Sing to my family.
Sing to the birth of us.
Sing to the birth of the one that will be born to us.
Let the union begin.
Let us slip and move beyond the slop that
creates uncertainty and calamity.
Peaceful bliss,
Less shit.
Now that is a Dream!
Oh, I cannot forget to include the stars in the mix.

Hey, Little Sister, I See You

Hey, little sister, what do you know?
Hey, little sister, I can see your spirit.
Hey, little sister, when you stare at the new moon, do
see the Angel's eyes that are also nestled in you?
Hey, little sister, I can see you.
Hey, little sister, I know you can see me too.
Hey, little sister, you're perched upon a tree,
blanketed in sun and love for all to see.
Hey, little sister, the purpose is yours to me.
Hey, little sister, I remember your spirit.
Hey, little sister, it is bigger than you know.
Hey, little sister, sing along with me.
Hey, little sister, can you remember me?
Hey, little sister, you can see it too.
Hey, little sister, I can see you too.
Hey, little sister, I truly love you.

Hibiscus

Yellow
Bush to mountain peak.
See myself as I fly amongst the clouds,
Swooping, swooning, and absorbing the humidity.
See the waves rustling as they wash against my body.
Feel as it holds, wraps, envelopes and frees my spirit.
As once I nestled in the bottom, I feel myself begin to rise.
Arisen to the top to be seen in the flowers, buried in the softness
below our feet to the top amongst the fire and the waves.
Feel as I sail through the land and am absorbed into it.
Feel as I look into the eyes of those who came before.
See them nestled in this moment in time too.
Feel as my heart settles and hurts.
Feel as I return.
Remember.
Feel, as I know this is the Moment I have awakened for.
Feel as I touch the air with my heart and my tongue.
Feel as the wind opens itself and rustles
upon my hair, tickles my spirit.
Feel as the gift approaches, sneaking, peeking in the mist.
Feel as I open my thoughts and give this moment to the One.
Feel.
Feel.
Feel as the pique has hit the note,
Pinging,
Plunging,
Swooping,
Swooning.
Funny how these baselines travel to this pique,
not quite the same, but One and the same.

Highest Good, and Best Moment to Sit

Hearing it again, the moment my heart
opens, clears, sees and responds.
Today this murmur is lasting longer and is a bit stronger.
See it more than feel it,
Opening a bit more but pinching as I breathe.
So as I look upon more, I seem to be able to feel more;
As I open more, I seem to be able to see more.
Trust is today's word and sense;
I trust that the moment is this one.
This is an able picture instead of one that can be
opened by realistic thinking, so the stretching seems
appropriate as my heart needs to lead this one.
So the more pinching, the more able I am to see.
This trust envelopment is something that is flowing
like a glacier, slow paced, solid and clear, pure—
Not a gradual river, but a large mass awaiting its own arrival.
The trust in the pinching, newness and opening, and the
feeling is one that has been well earned over time.
This is a day I will and can enjoy with open, long breaths.
As I sit, I am tired, so I will rest and not believe that the
pace can be dictated by anyone but God himself.
I normally have rabbit stealth, but lately
it feels more like a tortoise pace.
With a slight side look to the difference, I know I
can keep to my journey and understand that
tortoises have teachings for our people too.
Breathing, resting, openness, happiness and sitting seem
to be on the bill today. I will trust and slowly follow.

I will trust the enveloping, unfolding and kissing of my life.
My heart is on time to do what I can do,
and it knows what I can handle.
I will sit in child pose and rest.
Today feels like a child pose day. I know that I can and do trust
my Higher Power to release me, aid me, and build and create
what is needed in this moment and the next for my highest good.

Home Just as Easy from Here to There

Trickle, tickle, missing.
See the waterfall, feel the land, see the land
kissing, locking and sliding into the water,
Encapsulated in heat.
Feel the envelopment, smell the flowers and taste the mist.
Holding to the soulful memory, playing with
that moment and then smiling.
Yes, the overlapping moment from this Vancouver
Island moment to a Hawaiian moment. Hmm, it is
interesting to border the two times, moments, scents,
smells, visions, sensations, feelings, happinesses.
Pivot, baby, pivot.
Pivot, tilting,
Tilting and not wavering, as I will be there. Heck, *I am there!*
I am working to get there to play with, enjoy and rejoin you all.
Feel it all, my people. Aloha. Home.

Home

Peaceful bliss. I sit upon this, but no more shit.
I laugh because one is a cheap joke; the other
feels like there is a lot less of the shit.
So as I sit upon a mountain top,
I have a clear-thinking,
Open-posture,
Well-placed moment.
Situated self and perspective, sitting.
Opening and open.
So much less to say.
Clear to say no more than *wow*.
I hear and see so much more now,
And the cool part is that it is frickin' awesome to
be placed within it and at peace with it.
So as I sit upon this mountain viewing this life
I am placed, situated upon bliss and creative
caked treats, creativity blissfully sitting,
Closing my eyes,
Opening them to see all that is here.
Time, work, this to that—it does not
much matter, because I am *Here.*

Hope, Kiss Me

Pulsing, wishing, bliss, kiss,
Pushing the sin of the kiss that is only occasionally missed.
Hear it peak.
See it open,
Peak,
Fall.
I try to reclaim it, but no one's home.
Hear it.
See it.
Less on the feel, which works great for this girl, as
the missed is best, not kissed in this Moment.
Hear the *New* touch my lips and breast, wrap
around my body, and caress my soul.
See as I wrap it within me.
Feel as it absorbs the new that is now Me.
New to new, sing to me.
New to new, let me envelop and caress
and Harness the Newness.
Let it glance to my left. For it I say, "Thank you."
Let me glance, and then let it go.
Let go of _____ and Sing.
Sing because the promise I made did not include this,
The dancing I did. I did not agree to be this. The
dance I have will be a dance with you, God,
One that allows the work to continue and the Love
to endure with little to no loss to me or to others.
Let the song breathe;
Let my life sing.

Let me feel again the completeness that was
in a moment cherished by my birth;
Let me remember and hold that feeling and let its
light guide, mould, wrap, surround and waft through
this time and sing to the new tune I vibrate.
Let the time stop to pay attention to here, now, with you, God.
Let me believe.
Let me see.
Let me cry.
Let me dream.
Then let me sing again,
Sing to the One that wraps around and sings to me too.
Sing the song that wraps around and aids all.
Let us sing to the tune of a dance we
already know and agreed to.
Let us Bounce, Bounce and Bounce again.
Hear me, God, and help me remember to stay true.
Let my Ego rest for a moment. Let me sit to sing with you.
Let me vibrate to the next me.
Let me hold my space and move to the next time
that will envelop us all and let the hope ring.
Let the hope sing to us all;
Let hope, faith and love aid our laughter with the One;
Let us sit solidly within and with each other,
and let me connect to God, as I missed—
Or is it I believe I miss when I never do?
Let me see that this is my moment, with and around you.
Hold me in those beautiful white angelic wings.
Wrap around and hold me a moment as I
sing, hum, and wait for more to come.
I need to rest.

I am here, but I need to rest a second and feel
the warmth that your angelic wings offer.
I can feel the pulse as it touches my face.
Hold me in this moment and heal what is left—
and pass it through, as I am ready now.

Imagining

Imagining the Light.
Holdin' the Piece. Letting open the One that sits within.
Cliffs peaking at the edge, straddling the
present, opening to the Future.
Smiling as the peaking is so open. I see the ocean
to my left, and the peaking to my right.
Seeing more room.
Smiling again!
Smiling as this created feeling peaks within
and opens more—but more of what?
Today the question is a bit of a, humm,
not the curiosity that it once was.
Feel the Me that peeks out and honestly
keeps peaking with you, Great Spirit.
Bounce me.
Bounce me above.
Connect.
Connect.
Connect and know words will not make, capture, taste it—
So hold still.
Hold and know that while you *sit*, it is already here.
No need to shift your weight.
No need to bounce higher with your own strength.
No need to continue to argue with loose air.
No need to foe fight with lost angels.
No need to believe that the struggle is permanent.
Now is the Moment.
Now is the Here.
Now is Now.

ME

Crunching, munching, chewing on this biscuit that
often tastes a little different depending on me.
Feel as I recapture a moment that seems to be the same but
that is often a new development that sucks shit in the moment.
So as I listen, calm down, stay to this
newness—I stay, and calm some more.
Glistening, shining, hoping, Believing.
Open, Mellow, Prospering and Believing!
So as the smile hits my heart, glances across my
lips, tickles my soul, let me sing to you, God.
I am here.
I see you.
Feel this Moment.
Wrap me in your presence.
Let me hold this space
And, well, let go of that one.
I am now ready.
I am now open to the next step that has already arrived.
I AM, and the trinkets that kick and piss can slide down
the back to a place that is no longer touchable.
I can giggle, I can acknowledge, I can release.
I am here, God.
I am where I need to be, and *I am okay.*
I am okay,
And more days than not I am perfectly on time to *ME.*

Meadow

Open valley,
Sun-kissed oceans to open, flowing streams.
The gold-basked, dew-filled reeds of grass.
The welcoming of the union graces the moment.
Feel the aroma, the conjuring into this moment
to fill the contemplative moment,
Sitting in openness.
My heart is solid.
Feel as the stomach can retch at the thinking,
pondering, posing of thoughts.
As I jump from here to there, it becomes clear—it is
clear—but I do not need to label it with a word, thought
or conclusion, as the answer is atop the clouds.
In this moment, looking is the point.
To hold promise in the moment, to be present and to believe,
Holding, and now moving to, the Present.

Of It All

A ride to me is best seen in the moment taken to create it,
Washing clean the moments that held little
more to see than newness to me.
So as I wash and clean these moments and peek
at the beauty nestled in them, I see, I feel.
Washed and watching seem to be the real moments.
Even as I type I know the moment is here and has arrived.
I can see and feel it, but what now?
The now seems to be the now.
Feels like a call upon the wind.
Feeling the wind upon my face.
Feel the wind upon my heart calling the lullaby that nestled
into it long ago and, well, just recently too—ha-ha. It's funny.
Well, the humour in the creation and the spelling out
of it allows me to giggle, because, well, it is humorous,
lending itself to hand me something special.
Tonight I am up late and cannot sleep, so I am interested in
what the words will mean, what will be said, but honestly the
words and the time do not seem to matter when I connect.
Thoughts of my sons come to mind. How I would love
them to be connected and know that they are.
See us on a cliff beach watching the ocean and
marvelling at it on a new level, with a new view.
The level of joy we can experience in this time and in this
place is how we know and can feel that we are connected.
The cool part is knowing that they can get
it at that deep level in that Moment.

Gratitude and humour are on the bill, along with
protection, honesty, contemplation and, well,
anything that is meant for my highest good.
Appreciation has sunk in at a deeper level,
and I can now open up to more,
Open to love and light,
Humour,
Gratitude,
Contemplation,
Love of it all.

On Time and Perfectly Anita

Clearing and thinkin', thinkin' and clearing.
In order, out of order, does not much matter
in the mix, but doin' it nevertheless.
So as I sit with this newness,
I sit some more,
Thinking of a friend and finding a pattern,
Feeling that once I am known, seen and
felt, it might be too much.
The chaos in this thought is thinkin',
Am I too much?
Did I say too much?
Back again to *Am I too much?*
Then back again: *Did I say too much?*
In this ferris wheel of thought, the winner
never bounces up to be the *Real Me.*
Protection, belief, not knowing all wrapped in a
smell of just not me anymore, but once again the
tape goes, *Am I too much? Did I say too much?*
The odd part is that while I write or even when I ask
myself, it does not feel *as real* as when I asked it maybe two
years ago. Now I know at a heart level that it is not true.
I am perfectly Anita.
I am perfectly enough.
I am not too much.
And I am perfectly Anita.
So as I smile and listen to the woman, I believe the old tapes
that inquire about something, well, different can sleep.
As I try to hold onto anything when I am grasping
the newness, I can just do the best act of *sitting* ...

So am I too much? Even as I write it, I can feel my body
transform, returning to an old place with my stomach
tightening (but not as much)—and I feel an *ew* feeling.
Now along with the lessened *ew* and lessened stomach feeling,
I can raise my eyebrows, push my lips together and resist
the thought and the body sensation with a little smile,
A knowing glance to my knower and a slight
nod to go, *Hmm, maybe not today.*
Maybe today I will make all these new facial expressions and
let those old tapes lie. Maybe in this moment I will *sit quietly,*
Sit in the knowledge that I can resist the
old and position myself in the new,
To Believe I am perfectly Anita—and well timed at that!
So while my self-esteem puffs up, as I reach out to
good friends, as I laugh at the newness in me, I can
become more settled and settle in some more.
Today, God, I can believe and I can smile.
I could keep pushing, but instead I will just *smile and wait.*
Better yet, I can sit with a smile, knowing
I am coming along just perfectly,
As perfect as being born Anita,
Developing each and every day in this life just as *on time* as Ever!

One Moment

Slurpin' and Slurpin' a tickle.
Graciousness and Gratitude tickles, nestles, held and allowed in.
See and feel its extent.
My heart is smiling,
Feeling and smiling more.
Feel the connections and hold this moment
with the space that grace holds,
One in one.
Feel it vibrate.
Feel it surge into this to that to me.
Feel as I open my eyes to a world that was always here for me.
Feel as I wrap within and know its borders.
I have reached me.
Feel as the moment does not pass. This is the opened moment.
I can hear you.
I can feel you now.
I can see you,
The smile and that touch from my heart to all.

Opening Sunshine

Peeking into this space,
Staring into a Star,
Glimpsing the Universe,
Tasting the Sun,
Opening to this One Moment,
Creeping into the newness of this Moment in Time.
Feel as I absorb and, at times, pull back.
Feel as I honestly believe I am arriving.
Feel as I absorb and open to the lustre of this expanse.
With the use of thought as a tool, I find
that the experience becomes clear.
When dabbling too much in the *word-determined
perspective*, I can feel that pulling-back sensation.
During this time I can intellectually base my
mind on the perspective of Peace.
I can envision myself at the edge of a lake, with the sun
shining, calm water, and a light breeze blowing.
And like the wind my breath is soft, calm,
subtly paced and peaceful.
As I imprint this sensation into my mind, I can begin to sing,
To sing myself, to hold this Moment to me and to
begin to pray for my next moccasin step—
The next step that reaches me to the stars, to
the universe, and then back to me,
Praying, bowing my head, calming, and opening
my heart to the potential that is here.

Opening to You

Looking vast, seeing high, believing and bouncing from below.
Feel the earth below my feet.
Feeling the meadow of my existence; gazing at the
ocean with the wonder of a determined little one.
See this.
Pray about that.
Bellowing about this, believing less of that.
Seeing and feeling this and hoping for that.
Wishing for this and opening to it,
Wanting to not want what is not mine.
Wanting to stay open and to create the space that is one,
A path that runs to you.
To sit and to believe that the pain, the belief in this earth-
based time, is the point, and then I start to write. Then I
start to giggle. Next I see the brilliance that runs through
my children's lives; then I see the river running to you;
then I see those sparks in the sky that light me to you;
And then I believe that this one moment
is my connection to you.
It is the words, emotions, thought and careless acts
that allow me to believe that it is the point.
The funny part of my writing is that it is
becoming more abstract, which makes sense,
as I am most at peace in abstraction.
It is a newness that is settling into me now,
A belief that I am in this moment, in this time. With
you, that is honour, that is right, that is the point,
The point to me from you back to me.

So when I am thinking or feeling my way, I can rest on my
haunches and believe that I can still believe in the stars, enjoy
my children's laughter, sing with myself, sing into the next Me.
Listening to and seeing our people and loving it.
Feel that this point from me to you is the point.
Feel as I taste it, learn through it and let go
of what I believe to be the concrete,
So as I pray the point is the point.
To sit and enjoy the flowers around me.
To believe that I can settle, that I can love this
moment, and to know that the next will come
at its own leisure and in its own time.
Sit and live rather than sit and wait.
I guess this or that. It really points to the same solution,
which is to live in the best way possible in a Life's Moment.

Open Like a Grounded Lotus

Opening, blossoming, adjusting, reaching … more.
Sitting on this petal, rooting myself to the
depth that is my gratitude, *root*.
As I float on this leaf, my bare feet planted,
my found treasures nestled, I breathe.
I breathe the breath that is mine to take,
The one that transcends this era and plants
me in a new garden of time,
A time that now mirrors me in this one,
One that skips past the bullshit and allows me to smile at it all.
It is a reminder to look closely at myself, to treasure
the moment, the one that opens to me one petal at a
time so that I can envelop the potential in myself.
So as I sit upon this petal, my feet up now, feeling my
groundedness, my purpose, in this moment I breathe—
Breathe, taste, smile, and greet myself.
Greet the moment that meets this new Moment that is now here.
Feel it, revel in it, Enjoy It!

Position to the Tale, to the Day

Poised, positioned, able.
Able to rekindle, poise, position, Create, Amass,
Declutter, but those fuckers are sticking.
Old tools feel like the freedom I seek to further myself from….
I am used to relying on old ideals that do nothing
to help me cope except to say, "Buck up."
Feels like the cowgirl in me has switched to a tree
with a breeze nestling into its branches, which seems
to be the direction I am now approaching.
Hearing the old, sitting in the new; the
contradiction is hard to sit in.
While I adjust, I Trust.
I trust the path is laid for me.
It matches the space I am creating for the more subtle me.
I, at times, feel the need to kick, scream, absorb—
today not so much, as I don't want to keep doing it.
I want to sit by a bush, be supported in the grass, enveloped by
the protective, subtle beauty that is our Mother, and then *feel*.
It is a hard word when all I want to do is bolt, release, release,
release, but right now it hits my stomach, throat and chest
with a constriction that makes it hard for me to breathe in.
Working hard to sit,
Working hard to sit,
Working hard to sit with it.
So the witnessing I am doing needs to be that, a
Witnessing of the Pain, which is hard to do, because the
file in my brain says, "Fight, flight or freeze."
The spirit in me says, "Soul."
An enduring wash, peace nestled to my Mind now.

"Soul."
Letting the process happen with the
knowledge that I am a spirit.
The thought feels like I am touching it with my fingertips.
It is not quite integrated in this moment, but I
can have F*aith and Trust* that it will be.
Letting go of an old Belief is the ass kicker right now,
Trusting I can flow with this is the ass kicker.
Letting the feelings come with their own volition is an ass kicker.
Feeling the hurt in my chest, throat and
whole body is the ass kicker.
Sitting with this numbness is the ass kicker.
Wishing for my "normal" back, the time when control of my
day was not dictated by a fuckin' feeling, is an ass kicker.
So as I sit here knowing that the Ego and the Pain can sit
while I await the next level, which might be an honoured
one, I hope that it will be what I really want, but, fuck,
it is the waiting that is the hardest, the absorbing and
evaluating (or is it a belief that I need to do nothing
but be present in the process that feels more true?).
So off I go to sit by the ocean and ask my
Angels, my Guides and God to help me,
Help me to see,
Provide me the needed clarity,
The strength to sit within,
The ability to absorb without arrogance,
impatience, or malice to myself or others,
The ability to not feel so fuckin' choked,
Choked in this Moment with no fuckin'
map, as the old one will not work.
I must have Patience that the Map has
arrived and, well, is already here.

This sucks ass.

This sucks so much fucking ass that the taste
of shit is getting fucking annoying.

So as the rant almost touches my humour
button, I feel almost a smile.

A good start.

The cool part is that the start is already here.

The *illusion* is that I think I am starting, but I have
been preparing, shaping, shedding and being Present
for myself and the process, so I am okay.

Today is the day, Anita. *Please breathe.*

Please remember the time is the time with no extras.

The funny thing is that I want the lullaby now, the washing
of it from me, the disentanglement of its mass/presence. I
want the newness Now; I want this to not sit so fucking long;
I want the taste of shit to get out of my mouth; I want the
detox to go a little quicker, but, alas, this is the Moment.

God, I am here.

I will say, "Please support me," but I know I Am Today.

 47

Pray, Sit, Sun, Stars
and Awareness

Passing over the cliff,
Seeing the clouds, the mountain peaks.
Direction set, peace set, autonomy set!
So the peace settles and nestles into my being, my soul,
a blissful hibiscus blooming, a fragrant heart.
Feel as the stamping has subsided.
Feel the rush slow,
Slowing to a normal speed,
One that hits with smiles and laughs and a stream-like speed.
As the opening keeps opening I smile, gracious and grateful.
I smell the mountain tops as their fragrance
wraps itself around me, my Being.
I feel like the hibiscus is opening to the light, to me.
Opening, opening, opening more now.
So as my cheeky self smiles, so do my heart and soul.
Feel the butterfly of my being branching out more.
Feel the wings stretch and collect their strength.
Feel as the One nestles with me.
Feel as I am enveloped into Source.
Feel as the lotus, which has peaked, rests above the water now.
Feel as its fragrance is nestling into me,
soothing the bear that rustles within.
The bear is curled, resting.
Strength has arrived.
Feel as the fog holds itself to me. Sunlight upon the stars hits
above the mountains, breaking the fog, diminishing it.
Stars perched.
Stars show the way.

Funny, I sense that this is where I am from too.
The sun is like the stars but has a different purpose, showing
that it is Time, that I am Here and that I have *Arrived more.*
Feel my blossoming heart unfolding more out of
the Rubik's Cube that feels too much like an
incomprehensible puzzle.
Now with the plan, aid, direction, rest and
sleep, I am here full force. Open! Ready!
Feel the next beautiful step with my bare feet.
Feel the sun, knowing the stars share the night,
and feel my open, blossomed heart.
Awareness has arrived.
So as I sit with the Sun, the Stars and all that
is Here, it is Now Time to pray, to Sit.

Rainbow Light

Sing into the wind.
Open your eyes.
Blink away the sleep of generations, of cursing, abusing,
self-loathing and negative inner self-reflection—
It is purity to know what you can do and to be *a Rainbow*
Reflective to light,
Colourful in presence,
Brilliant,
Exciting.
Stand out with simplicity, honesty and presence.

Rekindle

Swishing, swishing, swishing and spiraling within,
Touching upon the gift and seeking the Peace.
Announce my death in a wish upon a tree.
Feel as it comes upon.
Feel as the swirl is complete.
Feel as the swish is now the swoop.
Feel and feel it fall upon my being,
Being upon this star, reaching up on this
mountain and sliding down this trail.
Trail and trail and trial,
Trial upon the open mind but swooning upon
a wish that nestles upon my heart.
Feel as the whisper is the roar.
The roar becomes the voice that slept its time and is now awake.
Feel as the shift becomes known and is clearer to my *Now*.
Keep grasping with my human tongue.
Keep reaching to taste it upon my lips.
Feel it in the air, but so unquestionable is
the taste that I continue to thirst,
Thirst for the knowing. And now I sit,
Sit upon this white leaf,
Sit upon this massive white flower.
Feel the droplet touch my tongue.
Feel as I transform into the veins that are
fed with this humid blanket.
Breathing in more now,
Settled and perched, awaiting the moment.
The moment is here.

It is funny to describe this *here* when it has been nestled within and is now aligned as if it has always been here.
Now upon this petal, soaking this juice called Life, I align myself, settle some more,
Resting now.
Need to rest and soak versus seek and destroy.
Rest upon your petal.
Rest, recoup, rekindle upon your leaf.
Believe now,
Believe in the Plan.
Show up for.
Show within.
Create silence.
Meditate.
Connect and *Relive* Now.

Riding to You

Swimmin', kissin', hittin' and at times missin'.
Cursing and then saying,
Cursin' and then singin'.
Swishing.
Singing.
Living.
Loving.
Healing and singin' some more.
See you.
Taste this.
Watch that.
Hold this.
Let go of that.
Draw circles around all the *musts* and *must-nots*.
Hear that this is not, and wish for not
Holdin'. Wave as I wash over its mound.
Sail to the known and feel the known.
Awkward? No.
Feel this and feel off with that.
Sitting calmly, feel this place, feel this
moment and feel the light pulsing.
I am now aware of it and feel it blossoming in my body.
Feel the sensation reachin' to my own space.
Feel it.
See what I want, and allow the space to move
with the knowing. Here is perfect too.
See myself riding a wave, surfing.
Feel the weightlessness in love and in life.

Feel the connection to the One.
The thinking has stopped. Feel the wave. It is *Acceptance*
Curving on my board now,
Smiling as it hits and
Hits again.
The shift of me to You is neat.

Sand in Odd Places

Connecting is at times a flawless, effortless merge, but at
other times it is like trying to stick yourself to sand,
A little grainy and equally uncomfortable.
I started with online dating again, or should I say online
looking, which is an interesting task/experience.
I've seen everyone who might be a match. I find
that the experience is just that, an experience.
See these amazing men. Like a beach bum trying
to merge with the sand, I end up feeling like I am
trying to merge where it is not quite possible.
So, off and on, the search continues.
It sometimes feels like when I see the men's profiles, I am
probing to see if it will be a connection. At other times, I
am stepping back to explore the reality of a connection.
Both are more neutral and less dramatic than before.
Today the sand does not rest in the odd body cracks and
places, but instead it sits warm and solid below my body.
I find that the layers I look at with these men make any
man not a match, even if I tried to weld him into one.
I find we can suit ourselves up so much that our true
nature is buried under layer upon layer of other stuff,
from clothes to beliefs to everything in between.
I just miss the fact that deep down we want
to connect, even just as humans—
A human, a spiritual peek with no
expectation of more than just that.
It feels at times that the layers do not make sense
when they counter who we are, which is One
and innately Connected to one another.

So as the pondering and looking goes on, I can
peek and enjoy, doing nothing more than that.
And the one who will see, and be comfortable
with himself, will connect with me.
"Toodles" is all I have to say to the rest.

Self

Light, Bright Mountain.
Meadow, valleys, pillows of potential nestled in me.
See the bellowing of the New as it kisses my cheek.
See the time that is Now.
See the one who kisses me too.
As the voice reaches mine, it sings to the sky,
the stars, the moon, the Earth and me.
It shares itself so well as it nestles into me.
As I feel the tickle, I smile.
I smile as the sun graces my face.
As I close my eyes, it fills those places that felt blank.
Now the evolution has come full circle. I can feel its etching now.
What was hidden has now shown itself—
It has enveloped me so subtly that the smile that now graces
my face is matched with my knowing that it is T*ime*,
The time to feel the sun on my face,
The time to share and praise the time that is Now,
The blue is kissing the red and pink hues above the mountains.
As I look, I wonder.
The purity of it is now complete.
I hear you now.
I can feel you now.
I can feel you now, the completeness of it.
The wondering can now sit by my feet as you swirl around me.
You touch the lightness in me.
I smile.
I smile at the lustful creation of beauty, of only
one who has been graced with purity.
I look over with a glance that shapes me now.
I am Now.
I am Now.
I have arrived!

 57

Sit

Where do I start?

How do I view this new information?

As I sit here, my chest feels full, my heart feels full, my
stomach feels full, my mind feels full, my being feels shaky.

My twin sons, what can I do to prevent my own ignorance, my
yearning to hurt you so that you cannot be hurt by others?

As ridiculous as it seems, that it what I
resort to when afraid, unsure.

It has now been confirmed that you are CYSN
youth, and as adults you will be a CLBC adults,
but what the fuck does that mean to me as your
mother and, more so, for you and your future?

This lack of knowing and my lack of surety is something that
pinches my being as I treat you, unknowingly, like fools.

I do not know what to do, or say to myself or to you,
which makes this spot that much more uncomfortable.

I am afraid.

I am scared.

I have no surety beyond knowing that you are loved.

You are both loved so much.

You were born in so much beauty.

And you were born for a Higher purpose—and for me right
now. I know that your path is teaching me to sit. I am learning
how to sit, and to sit some more, each and every day.

I will learn to try and will teach you so
that your value can remain intact.

I will sing well wishes and love praises to you, my twin sons.

I will sing to your beauty and to this moment.

Today I will sit less in resentment, as I do not know what
is going to happen. That uncertainty scares me.
I will sit today, tonight and in this moment, and I will Pray.
I do not know what to do, Great Spirit.
I do not know what to do except to *sit*.

The Mountain and Me

Mountains, snow covered,
Placed, nestled, with a peak that stretches
to touch the Heavens, the Sky.
Hear the sound of our ancestors speaking in the wind.
What do they say?
I can feel their subtle teachings as my
heart rests nicely in my chest.
It is not preoccupied; it is open.
I can hear you.
I can hear your soft words touch my Spirit.
I can feel the next sensation that is to be Me.
I walk another mile up the mountain and I pray some more.
I pray for strength as my being squirms
with the knowledge of the next Me.
As it shakes and moves, the discomfort
hits me and moves some more.
Knowing the change is coming and feeling the
energy transform the one that was once Me;
Knowing that I am here and knowing that
I am learning more and more.
I feel the need to continue to sit,
To sit and believe quietly that it will shift.
The slowness of the shift is the challenge as I squirm some more.
As the moment passes, I feel the next peace,
which I sought so hard to achieve.
Now as I can feel more, I know it was worth it
to touch to newness, worth the miles achieved,
worth the song that was sung to my newness.
Today I hear.

Today I am willing.
Today I can hear so much more, so I can do
what I was born to do in this life.
Today, God, I am willing.
Today, God, I do see the mountain, its challenges, its
blessings and the love that nestles it all within and for Me.

This to That

Wishing, bliss, kiss, hear you.
So what do I feel?
In this moment, contentment.
Contentment, connection, love, lust, calm.
Sitting in the ocean as I watch my being hit the
crescendo of this to that, from me to that!
Shock!
Not very surprising that the little piece of that fits with this and
jumbles into that kiss from me to you, and then from this to that,
Laughing as the juggling hits a moment that created Me.
Smart, that Creator, the Divine, the life force, the
ultimate, the One who flowed that, allowed me to
miss that, pushed in this, aided in honouring that,
cherished in this for this to that, from me to that!
Who knew? Honestly, not this little woman. But
the plan that was created in bliss and shifted
from that is one that is here—and it is now.
The pressureless bliss is one that creates time.
Time to dream, hope, pray, experience, live life,
taste space, hold this and let go of that.
As I sit, the core of what drove me is sleeping, releasing into the
Universe, becoming clear and becoming less of what I once was.
Sitting in this Moment, feeling Me.
Settling into myself, looking inside myself and
realizing that the content/calm space is Here—
The time worked, the moments cherished,
those worked in/through were worth it.
This contentment was worth it.
Feel more.

Taste more.
Laugh more.
Smiling with a little more cheekiness,
and feeling more content too.
Unplug another button.
Feel the evenness of it all.
Feel the peace wash over and within me.
Feel the love released from this to that, from me
to you, over that from this and back to that!
This to that, from me to you,
From you to me,
From this to that,
That to this, from here to there,
Spacelessness and an Open Life.

Three Twin Stars

Maybe the glimpse is that I am a mother, not someone
who is "making it", a martyr in this life or one who is "left
with these children", "strapped with this responsibility"
or burdened with all this stress and these extras.
Maybe instead the glimmer is my life,
One held with these three wonderful children.
I am one who is strapped with great kisses,
hugs, admiration and unconditional love,
One who is more with this honour.
It is the topping to this wonderful life and
a treat in this time and space.
It is a gift to walk alongside these three remarkable
young men whom I call my sons.
Matthew, Colbie and Alec, it is an honour to be blessed,
kissed, held, loved and cherished by you, to laugh
alongside you, to continue to learn with and from you.
Love to you, along with continued teachings and joy.

Treasure Space

Sometimes the best thing you can do for
someone is to pray for them,
To pray,
To energetically pull them beyond the present
sensation, feeling, thought, etcetera.
Today I am calling for prayers.
Prayers.
So when I sit here in my almost perfect state, I can hear
you sing me a lullaby, one that holds me in the light
when at times I cannot feel, see or clearly taste it.
When I am sung to, I can feel the love, I can taste it, and I
almost always reattach to see it clearly enough once again.
So in this moment sing to me.
Sing to the Creator to hold me.
Sing to the ones who have passed, and live in this
moment to witness us and our births in the next.
I am, and I am listening.
My body hums some more.
Funny that instinct is nestled in our bodies, ever guiding us.
Equally funny is how I can resist my own body's direction.
There is a falsity in that maneuver or choice (more accurately,
"reaction") because I know my body is that place where I
can touch the Heavens, Life, Love, Completion and Faith.
To start is to Pause in that view, will and limited power.
The Pause can then be an experience.
Lookin' upon a vision—
See this pond, calm water, a bit of fog
with no bright sun to be found.
The coolness nestles in your bones as you look across,
Absorbing, sitting in this moment and sitting within this Time.

Feel this moment envelop;
Feel it almost consume. Then comes the
Choice to move beyond it,
The choice to see what it is, to breathe and then to let your
presence move with one energetic breath at a time,
The moment to sit calmly by that pond.
Then to feel your skin, your body and your mind being
moved slowly, patiently and lovingly along—
Feel myself coming back,
Slowly moving into this Space.
Feel the capturing to this time.
Feel the sensation, feel, taste, dripping from me.
Feel as I hold with one hand this Moment and
slowly let go energetically with the other.
Spirit, my spirit, I call to this time and moment.
I call to remind you I am here.
I call for you to see that we need to be here.
I call as I call, as I call.
No more waiting.
No more sitting in that time, because it does not wait
or pursue more than this Time and Space will.
My beloved, cherished, nurtured, creative, optimistic,
loving Spirit, Body and Mind, join and be One.
Be One and Sing this tune,
The tune to sing us to Us.
Come and let go.
Play, see, lavish in Light.
Create space, learn in space.
Treasure,
Bliss,
Laughter,
Light,
Freedom,
Trueness to Being.

See You

Sifting through a part of my heart that beckons more
from me, I also see a part that is starting to emerge.
An awareness like a box made of gold cradled in a
field with a tree, a meadow basked in sunshine,
Thinking of our people again and starting to see a
deeper part of the importance of *seeing them*.
I was working with a youth and was reminding
her to *remember* as she soaked in the emotional
intensity, the sadness, of her moment.
This moment reminded me of the Young Empires song
called "The Gates", which repeats again and again,
"You are not alone." I know that to be true, both in the
presence I offer these youth and in the hope of a future I
can see clearly where healing "chunks" are removed.
I can see how we can rest in this hope
and in the moment's stillness.
The work I do often sets me up to see people
and equally allows me to work my energetic
boundaries. It saddens me as I *see* these people.
I see their beauty, their fight and their will to overcome their
past, present and future visions that are often dark, unsettled.
As I am present in this pain, it bounces
and reaches into my space.
It is in these moments that I can hear them as clearly
as if they had spoken their history to me.
This emotional and energetic touch between
us allows a "lift" for them.
It is like a software share powered from one to another
As I see them now and remind them of a hope.

I can see the programming entering, being absorbed, and rewiring them, and then a stillness calms their inner toll that was once bubbling over, scratching, tearing and moulding them to a space that does not cradle their beauty.
As to this wiring, *remembering* enters. It reminds them of the future them.
It is a future that I can *see* and that is an offered *reminder* of what they can have.
Today I pray for our youth, their families and the workers who are sifting through the work, the history and the pain that is slowly shifting, moving …
I continue to keep trending softly and keep *replaying the energy* that reminds me to rest, pray and clear.
This energetic clearing and darn good boundary work allows me to remember that I am not alone.
I have help.
I have strength to see them, their present/future hope, and I also have a way to show them *how to feel* this belief.
Today I am grateful and aware.

Up and Ready

To think that as I twinkle in the new sky I see you.
To see how much I have become in a short time—a
mountain of a potential and a peek at a gift.
As I feel the newness and golden gift
wrap in and around me, I peek.
I get more than a peek; I get a wrap.
As it flows like dust and encircles me, I feel
the transition that at times can hurt.
The funny part is that it is not a hurt that I would
normally have but one that is indescribably present.
Watch as this one bounces up, this one tastes the
tickle, this one mixes with the loving, and that one
might not even directly know it is connected,
So is the petri dish of life that creates so
much more in me planned or a fluke?
I believe in the faith that it is *True, Real and
Created* with no fluke involved.
I am flowing with it so much. This does not
mean it is not comfortable, but I do get to taste
it daily and I resist it with less vigor.
I find the push is faster and harder now.
I find that when I am in it, I can feel the sensation now,
and almost always it is *known, proven and believable*.

Washes to Light

There is no right or wrong in it.
Timing is right in the when, the where and the how of it.
The place is the Space of knowing that the
peace will come in its own timing too—
Struggling to get it,
Handle it,
To find a handle in a handleless moment.
See the horizon.
Breathe in the state.
Sitting and acknowledging the hurt,
Seeing more above and within it.
See that this Moment is all I have,
Appreciating and learning.
Knowing I am Here *to see* this Moment,
Birthed to relive more of it.
See it and know that this will Pass.
It will breeze itself amongst me and my Knowing.
The only state is Acceptance, Cherishing,
Caring, Knowing, Sitting—
Sitting is the hardest in this Moment,
To sit and to not process.
But the funny part is that I am processing
whether I want to or not.
I see the friends I love and value
Honour their place in my learning. I breathe as they breathe.
Regulated by Treasured moments,
Breathing one sweet breath at a time and
feeling privileged to do that.
Feel, see, Sit.

Today sit is the one that makes sense.

I trust that my Angels, my Guides and God will provide the space for me to Breathe, a large or small amount at a time.

Feel.

Feel.

Feel.

Feel.

Feel some more.

Honour this and know it will come and surpass the Belief.

"Love and know I love you," God would say.

Love and Know you are loved—

Loved, Treasured, Cherished.

Sending love to God, Guides, Angels and Dad.

Rest and know it is well.

Know that what I sit upon is moveable and shifting,

Shifted to a plane that is now Peace.

It is a plane that can offer solitude.

Feel and know I am loved,

Know I was loved.

Feel and set myself Free.

I am settled.

I am loved.

I am cherished.

I am Known.

Peace.

Rest.

Live

Life.

Create a space that is more to all of it.

Feel Life.

Waves

Foaming, pulling, looping, singing into the sand.
See the love as it folds upon the earth, retreats and
pulls the smoothness into the rough rocks.
Open to pull the roughness that can at
times sits stuck within or on me.
See as I open and taste the sun, wind and salt.
Absorb it in me.
Create an orb of existence that surrounds
me and connects to you, God.
Great and small.
Pure and crystal-like.
Feel the need to describe it, but realize it is
okay with or without the description.
Feel as the wind brushes me.
Feel as the pull toward the old is now loose.
Feel as the worries, regret, self-pessimism and
more regret sits in my stomach and mouth.
But there is a *freedom* to choose different now,
There is a freedom to be *honest* now.
Feel the time has glided into place.
Honest to this moment.
Honesty in the time and *to be gentle.*
As I feel you, Great Spirit, I am known, aware,
physically and spiritually present.
The mental and emotional are here too, but
they are resting in the moment as well.
Rest, love and peaceful connection.
Sit and wash over me, Great Spirit.
Pull what is needed to remove the old and insert the new.

Ready, able, capable, willing and honest.
This moment, this time, this space, an
open, honest heart and time.
Time to nestle and hold the Opportunity,
to release with your aid, God.
I am open and willing with my Angels',
my Guides' and God's help—
Grace, Willingness and Peace.

Beach

Through golden grains of sand is how my life has enveloped
me, making me into the Beach I have become.
I cannot believe the amount of shaping, moulding,
smoothing it has taken to open this granite rock, to
become the *soft, safe and warm place* I have become.
With each bright new sunrise, I shine amongst the
froth, the foam, the warmth of the ocean's lapping.
I have become the solid Beach I never knew I could be.
It was and is a great plan,
A plan designed and written in the stones,
in the Stars and in my soul.
How great a plan it was that I did not see it written. I never
saw it fully executed, but I have sure felt it develop me into
a trusting, open, patient, learning and spiritual being.
Today I will hold the ancient stone's beauty, hold the wave's
space, and allow them both to nestle and tickle me.
I *can see you* now—
I can see how great the Plan was, and I am surely open to
see what these next grains of sand shape up to become next,
because as I sit I realize that this is a pretty good spot.

Home to Centre

The mind and the pieces littered in it seem to fit
and get a little off-kilter, but the odd part is I never
truly notice their distortion in the moment.
As I sit here, I am in the process of truly
intending to write my first book.
This is a beautiful spot, a gracious spot, well timed.
Well, the book has been put out to two people whom I
absolutely love, cherish and trust, who have been on my
Anita Cheer Team (yes, we have a name—ha-ha).
Today as I sit here, I feel an astonishingly
special level of curiosity.
It feel curious because this is a thing I have worked to
achieve, to master, which is Me, little ol' beautiful me.
I have had the grace of God to aid me, friends
to cheer me, Angels/Guides to guide and
protect me, and a family to witness me.
As I sit here, I am unsure what I should do, but even
as I write that I am solid as shit about what I am to
do, so I am having an inner giggle. I write this as a
gracious fuck-you, one not directed toward anyone or
anything, just as triumphant "fuck you", I suppose.
It is paired with a "thank you".
It is an expression of thanks that I had all of those experiences
that grew into these magical, soul-gifted teachings and feelings.
It is the Peace,
The acquired, gifted Peace that shows me that I am alive.
As I tickle the world and it graciously smiles
back at me, my Heart is resting.

It is resting from the journey. I am sitting on this rock
that is cradled in our Mother's love and nurturance.
I am well.
I sit here as my Heart sings and expands. It
reaches to my Creator, to the One, to Us, to
Everything, and then it circles back to Me.
And Me,
A Smile,
A glorified smile back.
Smiling.

Printed in the United States
By Bookmasters